FOR MY LOVE

EVERY LOVER CAN RELATE TO

KAUSTAV GHOSH

Made with ♥ on the Notion Press Platform
www.notionpress.com

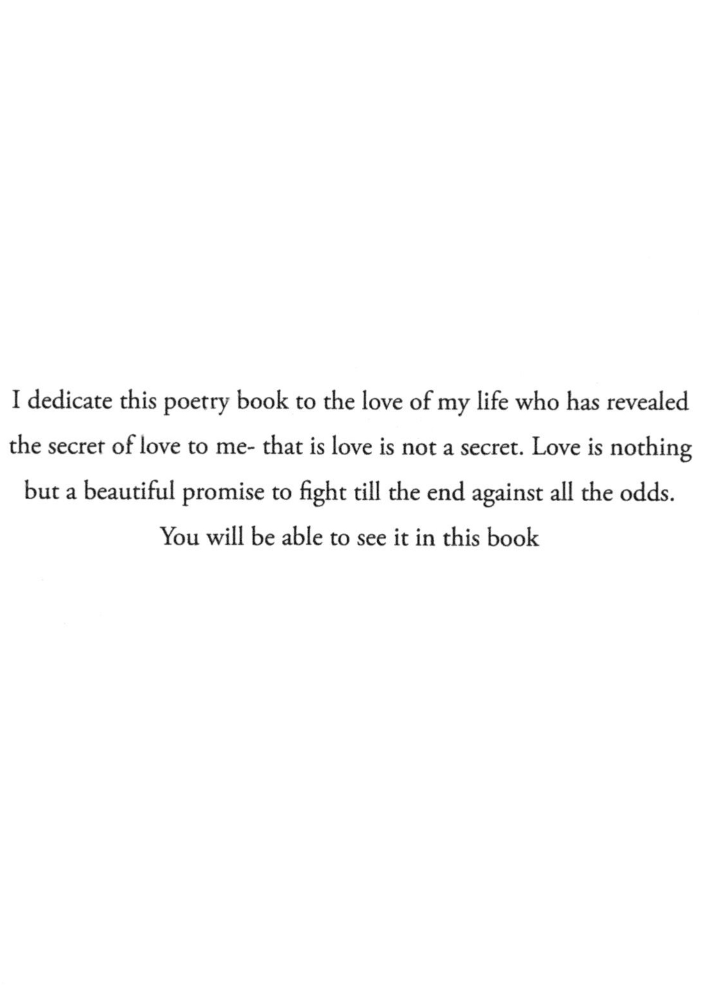

I dedicate this poetry book to the love of my life who has revealed the secret of love to me- that is love is not a secret. Love is nothing but a beautiful promise to fight till the end against all the odds. You will be able to see it in this book

Contents

Foreword

A book every lover can relate to. Lover means who wait till the end, who never give up till the whistle blown.

Acknowledgements

I dedicate this poetry book to my ‘R’ factor

1. The Struggle We Had

Till I remember that struggle-
That struggle we had,
The struggle we still have.
The struggle we face.
Then it was a struggle-
To see you at least in a month,
To see your face in a year.
Too see your smile.
Then smart phone was a distant dream for us.
To make a call,
You took your cycle to drive to the phone booth.
To say love you was tough.
14344, 234 was that code
or
To say te amo,
or anything by which,
I can say love you.
Be it in french, German or any other language.
I love you,
I really do.
I love you even if our luck took us apart.
I love you for everything you did to me.
I love you, I love you, I love you.

2. For You My Love

For you my love,
As you are my heartbeat.
For you my heart beats.
For you everyday is new.
For you my never ending love.
Thou my emotion,
my spirit you are.
Oh my love-
Everything for you, my love.
For you, for you, and for you.

3. THE STRENGTH

You,
Yes, you.
The embodiment of my strength.
The embodiment of my soul.
As thee are one.
Your smile works like fuel.
Who gives me immense strength,
Who never forced me but the force behind me.
The force of mine.
The strength which entangled in my body.
Yes you, that is you.
The Love of my life.

4. The Struggle Saga

Love itself a struggle,
Is not it?
In other sense love itself a jihad.
Even if two words are exploited together.
To spread the venom of hatred.
Love itself a struggle-
As it has to fight it out every day.
Fight it out against every odd,
Fight it out against caste, creed, religion and color.
Fight it out against every unreasonable norms,
Fight it out against every social evil.
And the struggle continues.
Even after at the edge of death.
Even after the Lord came to taught us love.
The struggle saga continues.

5. Dear Valentine

Am I too late?
Too late to wish you my valentine?
Love not for one day or month.
I fall in love with you every day.
Yes.
Every day, every moment of my life.
Oh dear valentine,
My love my life.
I life you, I life you, I life you.

6. The Answer

It was that time of my life-
That year of betrayal and heartbreak.
When my soul was bleeding.
But none could see it.
How to treat that wound which none could see.
The answer was you and your smile.
You came, you saw, you conquer my heart.
You healed me in no time.
You taught me the word 'love'
You came and complete my life.
You become the answer of my every wound.

7. True Friendship

When none was there,
You hold my hands like none other even think of.
When even my shadow moves into another,
You stay there.
Like an ever-lasting friendship.
You are there to talk when none was there to speak.
Yes, when none was there to speak-
Either speak for me or with me.
When there was cheating, betrayal and heart break;
When I could not trust myself,
I shared everything with you.
You listen to me, you heard me.
With the patience of billions of years.
Still I could not choose you for eternity.
Still I could not see you,
Still I search for human who can be seen.
Even after you make me realise you hear, you can be seen.
I forget that, oh dear I forget that.
I forget diamonds while search for gold.
I forget that self interest is the key which make people around you.
Forgive me my dear, forgive my weakness.
Its a promise to you I will wait-

Will wait for you till my last day.
Will wait for you till I got the salvation.
You will be in me, I will be in you.

8. Just One Chance

Its just a matter of chance-
A chance we ask for.
A chance we need to have by our side.
To prove ourselves,
To let the world know our worth.
Just one chance,
But zero conversion rate?
What will happen?
It will just make it hard.
It may take more time;
to reach your destination.
Keep working hard than thinking of missing a sitter.
Hard work is always worthy.
Just one chance-
Yet, many even did not get it.
To get a chance for which he is begging.
Either make it or break it.
Did not get the attention it expects.
Then dreams become despair at distance.
Then life become hopeless.
But when life makes you wait,
You should start making your life.
Only brilliant can make it, make it to glory.

You are the chosen one.
You will create history.

9. The Introspection

I don't want my soul-
To liberate and
to merge with the eternal brahman:
It is what I feel.
It is that revelation for this introspection.
I will come back again and again.
I will come back every time
I will not liberate till the last soul is liberated.
Thou shall wait this time,
The wait for a soul.
A soul's journey to its eternal bliss.
Though I have seen my soul,
The Introspection.
I have seen my soul by seeing you or
seeing you by seeing my soul;
May lord gives us the strength;
The strength to differentiate,
Differentiate between illusionary and ultimate truth.
The road to aretha,
Thee and thou same but different.

10. Speechless

You left me speechless,
I lost my voice.
Even that could not stop you.
That could not stop you to read my mind,
You could easily hear my voiceless voice.
When I lost my wish to live.
When I could not find a way.
You become the way of life.
You hold my hand tight.
The promise you made never to leave me.
Even though I scroll through your videos,
And it bothers me that you didn't scroll me.
You made me speechless every time,
My friend, my philosopher, my guide.

11. Journey

Life itself a journey;
Is not it?
This journey I am talking about-
It is something different.
This is a poetic journey of a poet.
Or may it is about a new born poet,
Or may be a poet took rebirth.
Whatever may be the case,
The journey just has started.
I have boarded the train towards my voyage.
My Voyage to excellence.
My voyage towards doing something in my life.
A journey of today's insignificant persons journey of tomorrow-
Contributing significantly for the people and environment.
Contributing significantly for humanity.
A dream yet to be fulfilled.

12. The Holy Promise

Promise-
How you mean it?
An oath wrapped with emotion.
A thing which is unbreakable.
Anything which breaks not a promise.
In this world full of treachery,
The inhabitance of traitors.
But everyone has a future which will come.
Which is more certain than the rising sun.
Which will definitely replace the old.
But not the new things in old wrapper.
Going with the flow not an option-
To choose or think of.
History teaches us-
To Introspect,
To learn and correct all the mistake,
To find out the missing puzzle,
To stop that never ending vicious circle.
They say history repeats itself,
But they forget to say one thing
History taught what to repeat and what not to.
Time has come to make a holy promise-
For our future,

For the future of our future.
To ensure safe, healthy and secured life.
So they can keep smiling.
That smile may never fade away.

13. To be or not to be

Destiny and destination-
These two words are different,
But it is differently connected.
Is not it?
Why not?
Sometimes destiny tear us apart-
From our dream,
From our destination.
Sometimes the differences in our destination-
Makes it easy for the destiny.
To split down the middle.
Makes it easy for them to remain as a barrier,
or a hurdle you need to jump.
Sometimes you could not.
Sometimes you could do nothing but to observe helplessly.
Whether we will be together or separated?
As the tragic as the Hamlet-
"To be or not to be that is the question"

9 798889 756729

Printed by Libri Plureos GmbH in Hamburg, Germany